THE
WILD & GARDEN
PLANTS OF
IRELAND

Wendy Walsh 1989

PAINTINGS BY WENDY F. WALSH • TEXT BY E. CHARLES NELSON

THE WILD & GARDEN PLANTS OF IRELAND

With 99 colour illustrations

Thames & Hudson

To the artist: with respect and admiration. ECN.

Fine as lace and firm as Blake's engravings,
The paintings of a dozen Irish wildflowers,
One after one, hung cleanly on the wall.

My friend the country walker, botanizer
Reared in the gutted streets of West Belfast,
Called every one by name from memory.

Gibbons Ruark, from 'The Enniskillen
Bombing: Before it Happened' © 1999

Frontispiece: *Narcissus* 'Wendy Walsh'

First published in the United Kingdom in 2009 by
Thames & Hudson Ltd, 181A High Holborn
London WC1V 7QX

www.thamesandhudson.com

British Library Cataloguing-in-Publication Data
A catalogue record for this book is available from the British Library

ISBN 978-0-500-51456-6

Printed and bound in China by Hing Yip Printing Co. Ltd.

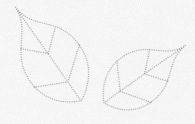

CONTENTS

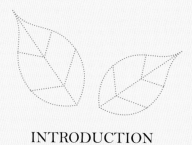

INTRODUCTION

The Origins of Ireland's Wild and Garden Plants

When the great ice caps that covered the northern lands more than fifteen millennia ago melted and shrank, the newly exposed land that now makes up the island of Ireland would have been barren, without flowering plants and ferns of any kind. Gradually, as the climate warmed, tundra plants crept in and started the process of colonization. Slowly, species by species, taller herbs, upright shrubs and the hardiest trees established themselves and created new habitats – forests, fens, moors and grassland.

Meanwhile, another process was altering the lie of the land. Melting ice led to a dramatic rise in sea levels, and the ocean swamped the continental shelf. Islands formed as the lowest terrain was inundated. When the body of water that we know as the Irish Sea was created, Ireland became an island, separated from Europe. To reach Ireland animals and plants now had to cross the sea; any species not able to make that crossing could not colonize the island.

There were no human beings in Ireland to watch the glaciers retreat during that remarkable period of 'global warming'. The earliest people that we know about were bands of hunter-gatherers who lived 'off the land', fished in the rivers and loughs and foraged along the coast for whatever they could find that was edible. They must have eaten wild plants: leaves, flowers, berries and nuts in season, perhaps some bulbs and roots too. Life was tough. Food was not always plentiful.

As our ancestors learned new ways of living, they began to change the landscape of Ireland. Agriculture was introduced around six thousand years ago and necessitated the deliberate importation of new plants. To create fields and garden patches, the eradication of native plants began on a grand scale. Trees were felled and shrubs and herbs grubbed out before crops were sown in newly formed fields. Barley and wheat were obtained from southern Europe – these species did not grow wild in Ireland. Cattle, sheep, goats and even red deer were also brought in – they did not occur as wild creatures on the island. So the natural progression of the island's fauna and flora was dramatically augmented by exotic animals and plants that could not reach an island by natural means.

For the next few millennia, after the first introductions of crop plants, the number of exotic species deliberately cultivated by the inhabitants of Ireland could have been counted on the fingers of a pair of hands. Growing plants for their beauty would have been unthinkable to our prehistoric ancestors, and even the cultivation of herbs for medicinal purposes or for flavouring the staple foodstuffs is unlikely to have occurred before the formation of monasteries during the first millennium of the Christian Era.

Once gardens were established in which medicinal and culinary herbs were cultivated, the expansion of the Irish flora began in earnest. Centuries later, gardens were formed, containing nothing but ornamental plants – vegetables, herbs and fruits were kept out of sight in walled gardens. To supply these 'pleasure gardens' with novel plants, thousands of non-indigenous species were needed.

Ireland's relatively mild and moist climate allows gardeners to cultivate a huge range of plants outdoors. We describe these as 'hardy', and there are many shades of hardiness determined by each plant's own ability to survive frost and dampness, tempered by location. Frost-sensitive plants can be cosseted in heated greenhouses. Plants which dislike excessive moisture can be kept dry quite easily. Thus ingenuity and technology have combined to expand further the botanical richness of Irish gardens.

Where did all these plants come from? From the wild places of every continent to start with, collected by travellers, some of whom were sent to faraway places specifically to hunt for unknown and untried plants. From nurseries, where selected plants are propagated. From plant breeders, who may be nurserymen, or scientists or just amateurs dabbling in artificial pollination. New plants can also arise by chance in gardens or the wild: a seedling with different characteristics; a 'sport' or mutation; an accidental hybrid.

We must also remember that garden plants are not always well behaved! How often have you had to weed out a plant, which you once admired and then planted, but which turned into a rampaging thug? There are many plants that produce prodigious quantities of seed, which enable them to escape, to 'jump the garden wall', assisted by wind, water, birds or other animals. Some plants were deliberately 'released' into wild places by farmers, foresters or gardeners. A large and growing number of these 'garden escapes' have found habitable spaces in the wild and joined the indigenous plants to enlarge the flora of Ireland. The list of exotics which are completely naturalized in Ireland is as long as the list of native plants, and includes rhododendron, fuchsia, butterfly bush, snowberry, Japanese knotweed, giant rhubarb, giant hogweed, Canadian pondweed, New Zealand willowherb and montbretia. They were all once cherished as rare exotics in gardens.

An Irish Florilegium grew out of an idea, originally conceived by Ruth Isabel Ross and Wendy Walsh, for a book of plant portraits, each subject having an Irish connection. Thus Wendy's watercolours portray a small and personal selection of the plants which grow wild in Ireland or are cultivated in Irish gardens. They were selected not necessarily because they are 'beautiful' – though most people will say that they are – but because we liked them and they had special botanical or historical interest. They illuminate the history of Ireland's indigenous plants and garden flora. The garden plants which we chose include exotic species that were discovered or introduced by, or were named after, men and women connected with Ireland, whether by birth or avocation. The cultivars (cultivated varieties) are of Irish origin or are somehow connected with an Irish garden or nursery.

For the titles of the original books we chose the unfamiliar word *florilegium* and to explain that I can do no better than quote the original authors' preface. 'Meaning originally "a gathering of flowers", its dictionary definition, "an anthology or collection of choice extracts", accurately describes the content of this miscellany.'

Author's Note

Wild and Garden Plants of Ireland includes all of the plates that were published in *An Irish Florilegium* (1983) and *An Irish Florilegium II* (1987) presented afresh in a new format to make these splendid portraits in watercolours available to a new and wider audience. The sequence of the plates has been revised, and new text and captions provided.

Since *An Irish Florilegium* and its sequel were completed in 1987, some of the rules governing the formation of both botanical (Latin) and cultivar (fancy) names have changed, so a small number of unfamiliar names are necessarily used in this new book. Also remedied is an error in the first volume; the portrait of *Rhododendron arboreum* 'Fernhill Silver' (Pl. 44) has been rotated anticlockwise so the main stem is more or less horizontal. Some of the published plates were composed from two separate originals; in one instance (*Anemone nemorosa*, now Pl. 34 and 94) the composite has been dismantled.

Only one plate is included here which was not in the original pair of volumes – *Narcissus* 'Wendy Walsh', a daffodil named after the artist at my suggestion in 1989.

E. Charles Nelson
Outwell, Norfolk, March 2008

IRELAND'S OWN

The standard list of the everyday names for wild plants currently contains just ten native plants which have the adjective 'Irish' in their names: Irish eyebright, fleabane, heath, lady's-tresses, St John's-wort, saxifrage, sorrel, spleenwort, spurge and whitebeam. There are also two recently invented names for alien species, escapes from cultivation, that are recorded from Ireland: Irish fox-and-cubs and Irish tutsan. There is also the Irish dandelion, but this is also called the Shannon dandelion.

The Romans called Ireland *Hibernia*. Thus, in formal scientific names, the Latin adjective *hibernicus* is used in combination with the names of the relevant genera to denote species which have links with Ireland. There are 'Hibernian' species of ivy (*Hedera*), hawkweed (*Hieracium*), bramble (*Rubus*) and whitebeam (*Sorbus*, Pl. 3), and subspecies of autumn gentian (*Gentianella amarella*), heath wood-rush (*Luzula multiflora*), lousewort (*Pedicularis sylvatica*) and common sorrel (*Rumex acetosa*) as well as two Hibernian hybrids, a sedge (*Carex* × *hibernica*) and a rose (*Rosa* × *hibernica*, Pl. 31).

There is another unusual and unfamiliar Latin word meaning 'of Irish birth': *eriugena* or *erigena*. *Eriu* was another ancient name for Ireland, and the medieval name Eriugena or Erigena was apparently coined on the model of Virgil's *Graiugena* (which means 'of Grecian birth'). Irish heath, long known as Mediterranean heath or *Erica mediterranea*, is now named *Erica erigena*.

The Latin name for the Irish spurge is an oddity. It is not clear why the great Swedish botanist Carl Linnaeus, who established the present system for naming plants and animals, chose to call it *Euphorbia hyberna*, for the adjective *hybernus* (the medieval spelling of the classical *hibernus*) usually means 'of winter' or 'wintry' – the word 'hibernate' comes from it. Linnaeus knew that this spurge, previously called *Tithymalus hibernicus* (*Tithymalus* being an archaic name for spurge), came from Ireland, among other places, and there is nothing wintry about it.

Irish heath, *Erica erigena* and *E. erigena* f. *alba*

Although it looks perfectly 'at home' in counties Galway and Mayo, well-preserved evidence deep within peat bogs indicates that the Irish heath did not inhabit these areas before the medieval period. Was this heather brought to Ireland from the Iberian Peninsula by medieval merchants as packing for wine bottles? The usual colour of the flowers is pink; white-flowered examples are rather infrequent in the wild but are much admired by gardeners.

Erica erigena (left)
Erica erigena f. *alba* (right)

2

Irish spurge, *Euphorbia hyberna*

Irish spurge is almost restricted to south-western Ireland, inhabiting shaded stream-banks, hedgerows and woodland glades. Although the individual flowers are green and inconspicuous, when in bloom the whole of the upper part of each stem turns bright yellow-green. The white sap exuded when the stems and leaves are bruised or cut is toxic.

3

Irish whitebeam, *Sorbus hibernica*

The Irish whitebeam is a small deciduous tree usually found in scrubby woodland in rocky places. As it is not recorded outside Ireland, it is one of the few native plants that may be classified as endemic to the island. The young, silvery leaf buds, looking like miniature magnolia flowers, are especially attractive.

SPRINGTIME BLOSSOM

While hardly a dozen plants are explicitly called 'Irish', there are reckoned to be around 950 native flowering plants and ferns in Ireland; for comparison, the combined floras of Ireland and Britain, including the Channel Islands, amount to approximately 1,500 species.

Given their different ecological requirements and botanical characteristics, our native plants vary greatly in their geographical ranges, abundance and, most noticeably, flowering seasons. The majority of flowering plants bloom between March and October. Very few plants are at their flowering peaks during the winter months from November to February. There are a handful of exceptions among the tiny annuals, such as common whitlowgrass and rue-leaved saxifrage, but these are not conspicuous and do not create a floral spectacle. For conspicuous and reliable winter blossom on wild plants, we must look to a scattering of gorse (Pl. 33) and the Irish heath (Pl. 1).

Of course, none of the seasons is exactly defined, and their waxing and waning differs from year to year and from region to region: spring will be earlier in the sheltered bays of County Kerry than on the Garron Plateau in County Antrim. Add to that the present-day trend of global warming, and the start of spring becomes even less precisely defined.

Be that as it may, St Bridgid's Day, 1 February, is by Irish tradition the first day of the spring. It was on that day that farmers began preparing to sow seed, and it was often marked by turning a sod or two in the fields. Soon afterwards you are sure to find the first blossoms on the blackthorns heralding spring.

Cowslip, *Primula veris*

In some localities (for example, The Burren) cowslips are still relatively common. However, in Ireland as a whole, the cowslip is much rarer than it used to be, and thus is a protected species in Northern Ireland. Cowslips make excellent garden plants, and can be raised easily from fresh seed.

5

Wood sorrel, *Oxalis acetosella*

Wood sorrel looks as if it should be nothing less than Ireland's national badge – the shamrock – but nobody wears wood sorrel on St Patrick's Day in Ireland. Numerous arguments, ingenious and daft, have promoted the idea that wood sorrel was the true, original shamrock, but the plant that has represented the mythical shamrock for more than two and a half centuries is nothing more than the particular plant the name 'shamrock' indicates, *seamair óg*, an Irish phrase which simply means 'young clover'.

Wood sorrel is a delicate and pretty harbinger of spring, and makes an nice plant for a shady nook.

Spring squill, *Scilla verna*

Spring squill was one of the first native plants recorded. It is confined in Ireland to maritime heaths and grassland on the eastern and northern coasts, between north County Wexford and County Londonderry. As it is a small bulb, it is ideal for growing in troughs or raised beds, and should be cultivated in well-drained, gritty soil.

IN PLASHY PLACES

The Irish climate is mild and moist; frost is never very severe, and snow rarely lies even on the mountain-tops. While rainfall varies substantially across the island, there is an abundance of fresh water and thus of plashy habitats. Plants which thrive in wet places, such as sedges and rushes, abound. Wild irises take over small stone-walled fields that can only be used for grazing a donkey. Reeds of all kinds encircle the loughs on which white or yellow waterlilies float.

The yellow flag or wild iris is one of the most handsome and abundant of our wild flowers. There are very few places in Ireland where this perennial does not grow, and it also makes a fine garden plant.

In complete contrast, the club sedge only ever grew at one place in Ireland and it is no longer a member of the Irish flora. A very rare plant might be thought difficult to please and hard to grow, but this sedge thrives in a friable soil and became a bit of a weed in Wendy Walsh's garden. As all her paintings were done using fresh, living subjects, Wendy was often able to propagate a plant after she had completed her painting. In the case of the club sedge, she had a rooted piece, a handy 'Irishman's cutting'.

Not so rare as the club sedge, yet a protected species which cannot be interfered with in the wild, the globeflower provided us with a challenge because we wanted to portray the native wild plant, not a cultivated one. Diligent enquiry led us to the late Mrs Michael Moody who lived on Rosskit Island in Lough Melvin. In her lough-shore garden, wild globeflowers flourished and she allowed us to have a plant.

7

Club sedge, *Carex buxbaumii*

Club sedge is extinct in the wild in Ireland, but does survive in a few gardens, although it is perhaps not an especially decorative plant. Discovered in 1835 on Harbour Island, Toomebridge, in the north-western corner of Lough Neagh, by 1886 the sedge had been almost eliminated from this habitat.

Yellow iris, *Iris pseudacorus*

Yellow iris occurs throughout Ireland wherever water is abundant. As long as its vigorous underground rhizomes are contained, the yellow iris is a beautiful plant for a bog garden or the margin of a garden pond.

Globeflower, *Trollius europaeus*

Globeflower is an uncommon plant in the wild, being confined to three north-western counties: Cavan (where it was recently discovered), Fermanagh and Donegal. The species is protected.

Whereas its natural habitats are places with abundant water, such as damp meadows and lough shores just above the high-water mark, the globeflower is easily cultivated in ordinary garden loam.

ON THE BRINK

Owing to the island's deeply indented coastline, Ireland's native flora includes plants that can tolerate the salt and wind which inevitably characterize coastal habitats. Displays of sea pinks (thrift) and sea campion splash rocky localities with pink and white blossoms, while bird's-foot trefoil and kidney vetch add bright yellow. On sandy shores other species thrive, and marram grass helps to bind the sand into dunes.

Sea pea and cottonweed are among the rarest plants in the Irish flora. Cottonweed is now restricted to the south coast of County Wexford. The species became extinct in Britain in the 1930s. Sea pea is relatively common along the coast of East Anglia, whereas in Ireland it is only securely established, at the present time, on a single beach in County Cork. Babington's leek is not so uncommon, yet it is largely confined to the environs of Galway Bay and Donegal Bay.

It is easy to grow Babington's leek in well-drained soil in the garden; the little bulbils which form in the flower-head make propagation effortless and fool-proof. Sea pea is also easy to cultivate as long as it is given very sandy, free-draining loam. Cottonweed is a bit more difficult – I only know of one gardener who grew it successfully and that was the late David Shackleton, who built a deep sand-filled raised bed for it in an unheated glasshouse. He also grew sea pea in an old stone trough, so that its tendency to creep and wander was curtailed.

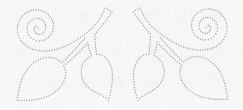

Babington's leek, *Allium babingtonii*

Babington's leek is a hardy variant of the wild leek, *Allium ampeloprasum*, which is widespread around the Mediterranean Sea. The flower-head contains about equal numbers of small pink flowers and bulbils, some of which are borne on long, slender stalks. Babington's leek was probably once cultivated for these edible, garlic-flavoured bulbils.

Sea pea, *Lathyrus japonicus* subsp. *maritimus*

Mature plants of the sea pea are exceedingly rare in Ireland. Yet walk along a western beach in winter, examining the flotsam, and you will probably find some sea pea seeds.

Where did they come from? The only plausible answer is that they floated across the Atlantic Ocean from North America. I grew the plant which Wendy painted from one such seed.

12

Cottonweed, *Otanthus maritimus*

Cottonweed grows on coastal shingle banks only in one place in the south-eastern corner of Ireland. The species was more widespread in the past both in Ireland and Britain. Cottonweed is a protected species. While its population in Ireland is stable, the shingle habitat is threatened by human activity.

THE BURREN'S
'ALPINE' PLANTS

The Burren, which is situated on the west coast of Ireland, to the south of Galway Bay, is renowned for its contradictions: for its barren rockiness and for its abundant wild flowers. The grey limestone imbues the landscape with a special luminosity, which, to my mind, enhances the colours of the flowers.

For more than four hundred years The Burren's reputation as a haven for plants has been upheld by the spring gentian, and that is still the plant which visitors most want to see. Yet there are hundreds of other species, and for spectacle it is hard to beat the mats of mountain avens, which occur even on the highest hills.

The Burren's enigmas also include the turloughs or vanishing lakes – full of fresh water in winter, but only grassy hollows in summer. The fluctuating water levels in a turlough present special difficulties for the plants that inhabit them, for they can be entirely submerged in winter, yet are high and dry in summer. Around the margins of some turloughs there is a band of shrubby cinquefoils.

Spring gentian, mountain avens and shrubby cinquefoil are not unique to The Burren; all three occur elsewhere in Ireland, but only in The Burren are they found growing in close proximity. They also occur outside Ireland, but only in The Burren can they be seen in the same patch of ground as plants which belong to more southern habitats, including maidenhair ferns (Pl. 16) and dense-flowered orchids.

While spring gentian and mountain avens are often called 'alpine' plants, this is not entirely accurate. You will encounter both close to sea level in The Burren.

13

Mountain avens, *Dryas octopetala*

Huge, glistening patches of mountain avens, a plant typical of Arctic tundra, carpet the lowlands and the limestone hills of The Burren. The white flowers are followed by distinctive fluffy clusters of plumed 'seeds', which are dispersed by the wind. In bygone times, the old woody stems were harvested for use as kindling.

Spring gentian, *Gentiana verna*

Spring gentian is the undoubted gem among the wild flowers that crowd the limestone pavements of The Burren and the Aran Islands. Nowhere else in Ireland or Britain is this diminutive flower seen in such profusion. The gentians are usually in their prime during the first two weeks of May.

15

Shrubby cinquefoil, *Potentilla fruticosa*

Shrubby cinquefoil has its Irish headquarters in The Burren. In some of its Burren habitats, the shrubs can be almost completely under water for part of the winter. The wild plants bear either male or female flowers, which can be distinguished by, respectively, the presence or absence of fertile, pollen-laden stamens.

A SECOND
BURREN TRIO

Maidenhair fern is delicate; it needs to be sheltered in a humid cranny. There are plenty of those in The Burren and the offshore Aran Islands, in the *scailps* (grikes) that crisscross the limestone pavement. Indeed, I always get a thrill when I am walking there and suddenly spot the fern's tell-tale fronds deep down in one of these crevices. This dainty plant will also grow where little springs of fresh water seep from cliff faces.

While the maidenhair fern is elusive and usually concealed, the harebell and bloody cranesbill are widespread and conspicuous in The Burren and on the Aran Islands. You don't have to seek them diligently; their vivid flowers are easily spotted. I have found harebells growing in the *scailps* on the summit of the highest of The Burren's hills, the flowers waving in the incessant breeze. Bloody cranesbills can form knee-deep hummocks where there is shelter up against the dry-stone walls.

Both Wendy and I greatly enjoy The Burren. After completing *An Irish Florilegium*, we spent several years working on a book which celebrates, in words and watercolours, the wild flowers of this extraordinary place, which many people find forbidding and desolate. Through the window of a tourist coach or the windscreen of a car, this is often the impression, summed up by the pejorative phrase 'a lunar landscape'. The Burren is for walking, for lingering, for botanizing on your hands and knees, slowly.

16

Maidenhair fern, *Adiantum capillus-veneris*

The maidenhair fern is indigenous to Ireland and is one of the characteristic plants of The Burren and the Aran Islands. The fronds have black stems, and fan-shaped pinnae (leaflets). Like all ferns, this species does not produce flowers and seeds. Ferns reproduce by wind-borne spores.

17

Harebell, *Campanula rotundifolia*

The harebell inhabits grassy places where the soil is free-draining and infertile. Thus it is a familiar wild flower on stable coastal dunes and on limestone pavement throughout Ireland. One of the harebell's Irish names, *méaracán púca*, signals the folk belief that this flower is protected jealously by the Little People!

Bloody cranesbill, *Geranium sanguineum*

Although bloody cranesbill occurs throughout Ireland in suitable habitats, the pale grey limestone rocks of The Burren seem to enhance the vivid magenta of its flowers. Peer closely at a single flower and you will notice that the anthers are turquoise. And, the leaves often turn scarlet in late autumn. Bloody cranesbill makes a fine and easy garden plant.

LUSITANIAN PLANTS

As exploration and cataloguing of the native flora of Ireland progressed during the first half of the nineteenth century, a pattern emerged of a remarkable group of indigenous plants that also inhabited southern and western parts of mainland Europe. These plants usually did not grow in Britain, and reached a higher northern latitude in Ireland than on the continent. They numbered about fifteen species and were mainly to be found in the south and west of the island. In 1866, David Moore and Alexander Goodman More listed these species: spotted rock-rose, kidney-leaved saxifrage (Pl. 21), St Patrick's cabbage (Pl. 21), Irish heath (Pl. 1), Mackay's heath (Pl. 27), Dorset heath (Pl. 26), strawberry tree (Pl. 19), St Dabeoc's heath (Pl. 25), large-flowered butterwort (Pl. 20), Killarney fern (Pl. 24), maidenhair fern (Pl. 16), Kerry lily (Pl. 23), Irish spurge (Pl. 2) and Cornish moneywort. Over the succeeding decades the list has been enlarged a little and modified, but these core plants remain. This group of species became known as the 'Lusitanian Element' of the Irish flora, although that term is now largely abandoned by plant geographers.

We can be certain that none of these plants grew in Ireland at the height of the last glacial period because they could not have survived the freezing conditions, yet how and when they reached Ireland after the ice melted are questions which cannot be answered definitively. Certainly, too, there is no one explanation that accounts for all the species because some, like the Irish heath, perhaps came here by accident, aided by human beings. The two ferns are most likely to have arrived as wind-dispersed spores. For the rest, migration over the continental shelf, when it was still dry land, is the least improbable improbability.

The search for explanations continues.

19

Strawberry tree, *Arbutus unedo*

The autumn-flowering strawberry tree has the unusual characteristic of bearing clusters of flowers alongside ripe fruits that formed the previous autumn. This evergreen tree, a member of the heather family, is native only to counties Cork, Kerry and Sligo. It flourishes around the Killarney loughs. Although the dangling fruits resemble strawberries, they are not as juicy nor as tasty. They are quite dry and gritty, in fact. Hence, perhaps, the strange Latin name *unedo*, which may mean 'I eat one' – only one!

Large-flowered butterwort, *Pinguicula grandiflora*

The large-flowered butterwort abounds in counties Cork and Kerry, even growing on bare rocks across which water continually trickles. It is relatively easy to cultivate, given damp peaty soil: James Drummond, curator of the Royal Cork Institution's Botanic Garden, was perhaps the first to do so early in the nineteenth century.

21

St Patrick's cabbage, *Saxifraga spathularis*, kidney-leaved saxifrage, *Saxifraga hirsuta*, and false London pride, *Saxifraga × polita*

Kidney-leaved saxifrage grows in shady places such as rocky gullies and on mountain ledges only in counties Cork and Kerry. It is an evergreen, rosette-forming perennial, distinguished from similar native saxifrages by its slender, hairy, perfectly cylindrical leaf-stalks. The more widely distributed St Patrick's cabbage is also a perennial which has flattened, almost hairless leaf-stalks. Where kidney-leaved saxifrage and

St Patrick's cabbage grow close together in the wild, they produce a hybrid called false London pride, *Saxifraga × polita*. This can be abundant, especially in southwestern Ireland. Mysteriously, false London pride has been found in a few places in western Ireland where the kidney-leaved saxifrage does not grow, suggesting that the latter was once more widespread that it is today.

Saxifraga spathularis (right)
Saxifraga hirsuta (centre)
Saxifraga × polita (left)

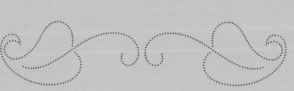

KERRY AND KILLARNEY

About three-quarters of the flowering plants and ferns which are native to Ireland occur in the county of Kerry. The 'Lusitanian Element' is well represented there, mainly due to the mild and moist climate. The county also has a wide range of sharply contrasting habitats, from rocky headlands to coastal dunes, and from lime-rich pastures to acidic peat bogs, with plenty of freshwater habitats and a long and deeply indented coastline. Ireland's highest mountains are in the county, providing an altitudinal range of more than 1,000 metres from sea level to the summit of Carrauntoohil.

According to a recent survey of the floras of Britain and Ireland, there are perhaps fifteen species native to Ireland which do not occur in Britain. Of these, ten inhabit Kerry, namely blue-eyed grass (Pl. 30), Irish spleenwort, Irish whitebeam (Pl. 3), Kerry lily, kidney-leaved saxifrage (Pl. 21), large-flowered butterwort (Pl. 20), recurved sandwort, St Patrick's cabbage (Pl. 21) and strawberry tree (Pl. 19). In 2003, to our surprise, Mackay's heath (Pl. 27) was also added to the Kerry flora.

To these 'specialities' may be added the Killarney fern, which is surprisingly widespread but not plentiful in Ireland and Britain. Its fame arose, and it acquired its name, in the middle of the nineteenth century because it was the plant everyone wanted to see when they visited the lakes of Killarney.

Hawkweeds are a difficult group of plants to classify and identify. There are more than two hundred 'microspecies' in Ireland and Britain, one of which turned up in a Dublin garden under a garbled name. This mislabelled perennial turned out to be Scully's hawkweed, which is a handsome plant and easy to cultivate.

22

Scully's hawkweed, *Hieracium scullyi*

There are numerous different hawkweeds native to Ireland and Britain. Scully's hawkweed, named after its finder Dr Reginald Scully (1858–1935), author of *The Flora of County Kerry*, is restricted to a small part of one river valley in County Kerry – it occurs nowhere else in the world. This species has been grown in Irish gardens since the 1980s.

23

Kerry lily, *Simethis planifolia*

The Kerry lily was believed, until recently, to be confined in Ireland to a stretch of coast in County Kerry, on the northern side of Kenmare Bay. However, the species is now known from similar habitats on the coast opposite, in west County Cork. It is a protected species.

24

Killarney fern, *Trichomanes speciosum*

The Killarney fern inhabits wet, dark nooks and small caves, often behind waterfalls. Famously and ruthlessly exploited during the nineteenth century as a plant for growing indoors in dark rooms in fashionable Wardian cases, this delicate fern was almost eradicated about Killarney. But *pteridomania*, the fern craze, dwindled rapidly and the fern still exists in its old Killarney haunts.

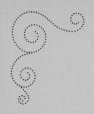

IRISH HEATHERS

Heathers have been a life-long interest of mine, but they are not the easiest subjects for an artist to paint: you need extraordinary patience to depict the myriad leaves.

St Dabeoc's heath is one of the gems of the Irish flora and one of the seven heathers that occur wild in Ireland. It has large, usually purple bells but sometimes plants with red or pure white flowers occur. *Daboecia* is confined to Connemara and south County Mayo.

St Dabeoc's heath is most unusual because it received its Latin and common names from a saint who lived more than a millennium and a half ago and who is associated with Lough Derg in County Donegal. When the Latin name was coined, an error was made and the vowels *e* and *o* were reversed.

Connemara is a heather 'hot spot'; there are five different species of *Erica* in the area, plus a natural hybrid which was thought until recently to be unique to Ireland, as well as the ubiquitous ling or common heather (*Calluna vulgaris*). The rarest of these heathers is the Dorset heath, and it may not be native. Mackay's heath is abundant in the area between Clifden and Roundstone where it forms a natural hybrid with the cross-leaved heath (*Erica tetralix*). Whereas the Dorset heath is not found anywhere else in Ireland, Mackay's heath, as well as the hybrid Praeger's heath (*Erica* × *stuartii*), are now also known from counties Kerry, Mayo and Donegal.

St Dabeoc's heath, Mackay's heath and Praeger's heath do not occur as wild species in Britain, nor does another Connemara heather, the Irish heath (Pl. 1).

The other heathers that are indigenous in Ireland are bell heather (*Erica cinerea*), which abounds in Connemara and forms a spectacular summer display with the dwarf western gorse, and perhaps Cornish heath (*Erica vagans*), which is confined to a single site in County Fermanagh.

25

St Dabeoc's heath, *Daboecia cantabrica*, *D. cantabrica* f. *alba* and *D. cantabrica* 'Praegerae'

St Dabeoc's heath is one of the glories of western Ireland. White-blossomed plants (*D. cantabrica* f. *alba*) were first reported in the early 1800s. The rarest shade is pure red: 'Praegerae' was found in Connemara by Mrs Hedi Praeger in 1938. There are numerous other wild-collected cultivars (cultivated varieties) of St Dabeoc's heath, including a double-blossomed one named 'Charles Nelson'.

Daboecia cantabrica (centre)
Daboecia cantabrica f. *alba* (lower right)
Daboecia cantabrica 'Praegerae' (left)

Dorset heath, *Erica ciliaris*

It is possible that the tiny patch of Dorset heath growing beside the 'Bog Road' near Roundstone in Connemara, in the far west of County Galway, is the last surviving remnant of a native population discovered by Thomas Fleming Bergin (d. 1863) in September 1846. It is also plausible that somebody planted this distinctive heather, thus 'forging Nature's fingerprint'.

Mackay's heath, *Erica mackayana*

Mackay's heath occurs in four separate localities in western Ireland. Elsewhere, this heath only grows in northern Spain. Although named after James Townsend Mackay (1775–1862), curator of Trinity College Botanic Garden in Dublin, Mackay's heath was discovered at Roundstone, Connemara, about 1835, by the local schoolmaster, William McCalla (*c.* 1814–1849).

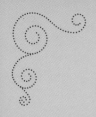

AMERICAN INTERLOPERS

One puzzle pertaining to the wild flora of Ireland is the presence of a few species which also occur, or have their closest relatives, in North America. The prime example is the pipewort found in loughs in western Ireland and western Scotland. How these plants can be native to temperate parts of eastern North America as well as to western Europe is not easy to explain by conventional views of plant evolution and geography.

Among the enigmatic North American species found in Ireland is blue-eyed grass – it is not a grass but a relative of irises. It is possible that the Irish plants are a distinct species deserving its own 'Hibernian' name *Sisyrinchium hibernicum.*

No mystery surrounds the extraordinary pitcherplant. This is a native of eastern North America, and it was deliberately planted on several Irish bogs in the late nineteenth century. Some of those pitcherplants survived and produced seed, and so the species became naturalized. While it is a fascinating plant with remarkable habits, the pitcherplant is not really a welcome addition to the Irish flora because it is an invasive alien.

To many people, fuchsia seems so 'at home' in Irish hedgerows that they pass it by without wondering why a South American, bird-pollinated shrub can grow 'wild' in another hemisphere. In the plant's true home, the dangling red and purple flowers attract hummingbirds, which sip nectar from the blossoms. While the shrubs blossom profusely in Ireland, they rarely produce seedlings, partly because there are no hummingbirds to make sure that the flowers are effectively pollinated. Thus fuchsia still relies on humans for its spread; almost any shoot stuck into the ground will produce roots.

Fuchsia 'Riccartonii'

Two different forms of *Fuchsia* occur in Irish hedges: both have escaped from cultivation. The one with slender, dullish red buds closely resembles wild *Fuchsia magellanica* from southern South America. The other fuchsia, the form that Wendy painted, has fat buds which are brighter red – they pop open when squeezed gently. It is a nineteenth-century garden hybrid, raised in Scotland, and known as 'Riccartonii'.

Pitcherplant, *Sarracenia purpurea*

The hooded, flask-like leaves – the 'pitchers' – of the pitcherplant are very effective insect traps. Like Venus's flytrap (Pl. 89), pitcherplants are insectivores, and gain some of their essential nutrients from the decayed bodies of the trapped insets. Pitcherplants are naturalized on bogs in several Irish counties, having been deliberately planted, first in County Offaly, around 1884.

30

Blue-eyed grass, *Sisyrinchium angustifolium*

Blue-eyed grass is one of the enigmas of the Irish flora – a supposed North American species with no close relatives among Europe's wild plants. For a long time its Latin name was *Sisyrinchium* *bermudianum* although the Irish plant is hardy and does not resemble the tender, larger-flowered species which grows in Bermuda. The flowers only open on bright sunny days.

ANCIENT NORTHERNERS

The Irish rose, Irish yew and Irish gorse – all three being cultivars (cultivated varieties) – arose as wild plants in two northern counties, Down and Fermanagh. The yew and gorse are unusual fastigiate (upright) forms. The rose was a hybrid. All three were chance seedlings.

The first gardeners grew plants which were not to be found in the countryside around their homes. If plants can be gathered from the wild when they are required for any purpose, there is no need to waste time, space or energy cultivating them.

Thus the first plants grown by Ireland's gardeners and farmers were exotics, and no one bothered about the natives. However, that changed in the eighteenth century. The very familiar Irish yew or, as I prefer to call it, the Florencecourt yew, arose in my home county, Fermanagh, during the eighteenth century, and by the early 1800s it was being propagated and planted. Its sombre evergreen foliage, and the melancholy mood that prevailed during the latter half of the nineteenth century, combined to transform the Irish yew into a funereal tree. It was soon being planted in every cemetery and graveyard.

The yellow-fruited yew probably arose around the same time – it is a pity that it is such a large tree, for the translucent yellow cup which enfolds the seed glows brightly on sunny days, making the tree sparkle.

The Irish rose was introduced into gardens from the wild in the last decade of the eighteenth century, and the Irish gorse was discovered shortly after the start of the nineteenth century.

31

Irish rose, *Rosa* × *hibernica*

John Templeton (1766–1825), a renowned naturalist and keen gardener, found this rose, to which he gave the Latin name *Rosa* × *hibernica*, at Holywood, County Down, about 1795. Its parents were the dog rose and the burnet rose. Urban development during the twentieth century overwhelmed the rose's habitat, but a plant was rescued and so this natural hybrid survives in cultivation.

32

Irish yew, *Taxus baccata* 'Fastigiata', and yellow-fruited yew, *Taxus baccata* 'Lutea'

The strictly upright Florencecourt, or Irish, yew is one of the earliest cultivars of Irish origin; the original was found on Cuilcagh Mountain near Florencecourt about 1740. The original mother-tree – all Irish yews are female – which has to be at least 260 years old, still grows in the demesne at Florencecourt. The yellow-fruited yew is also an antique cultivar; a tree growing at Clontarf Castle was propagated in the 1830s.

Taxus baccata 'Fastigiata' (upper)
Taxus baccata 'Lutea' (lower)

33

Gorse, *Ulex europaeus*, and Irish gorse, *Ulex europaeus* 'Strictus'

Gorse, also known as furze or whins, is ubiquitous in Ireland. Proverbs invoke it – 'When furze is out of bloom, kissing is out of fashion'. 'Strictus', with erect shoots and slender spines, was found about 1804 at Mount Stewart, County Down, whence it was brought to Glasnevin Botanic Gardens by the under-gardener John White (d. 1837).

Ulex europaeus (lower)
Ulex europaeus 'Strictus' (upper)

DOCTOR MOLLY

Dr Molly's Ishlan was a wonderful, ineluctable garden. It was always a joy to visit, and I never came away without a load of plants. Admire something or ask about its history and you were sure to leave with an offshoot. I did not have to ask: 'Do you think that plant might have a little brother?'

Dr Molly Sanderson (1913–1995) was a family doctor in general practice with her husband, Noel, in Ballymoney, County Antrim. Her very particular memorial is a jet-black perennial pansy, which was raised by a fellow doctor, Scott Stone of Margate in Kent. He gave it to Molly, who propagated it and gave its 'little brothers' to everyone.

I learned a lot from Molly Sanderson. She was a superlative plantsman, as generous with information and recollections as with plants. Among her many favourites Molly had a passion for wood anemones and collected all she could find – I obtained 'Lady Doneraile' from her.

Ishlan was also a last refuge for many plants that had become rare by the 1970s and 1980s. Molly kept alive plants that had ceased to be available in the trade, as well as plants which her friends had given her over the years and which she admired and cherished. The double-flowered primrose called 'Elizabeth Dickey' was one such cultivar of Irish origin which Molly had preserved, and it was in Ishlan, when visiting with Dr Brian Mulligan and his wife, Margaret, that I first encountered the old poppy named 'Fireball'. Brian, another superb Ulster-born plantsman, helped to unravel its history.

'The best way to keep a plant is to give it away.' Ishlan is no longer a paradise, but Molly's plants are still being propagated by many grateful plantsmen because she gave them away unselfishly.

34

Wood anemone, *Anemone nemorosa* 'Lady Doneraile'

This wood anemone was found about 1900 by the Viscountess Doneraile, perhaps in County Cork. The large, pure white flowers are exceptionally fine. Lady Doneraile (Mary Ann Grace Louisa St Leger; 1826–1907) was a keen gardener who, during the 1850s, obtained rare plants from the Royal Botanic Gardens, Kew, in exchange for samples of hand-made Irish lace and pieces of hand-carved bog-oak. Lady Doneraile's 'barter goods' are still cared for in the collections at Kew.

35

Papaver 'Fireball'

'Fireball' creeps. Out of control, this perennial, low-growing, multi-petalled poppy could become an ineradicable menace, according to Murray Hornibrook, a keen plantsman who grew it in the early 1900s. 'Fireball' originated in Mrs Matilda Webber's garden at Kellyville, Athy, County Kildare, during the late 1870s, although its parentage is obscure.

36

Primrose, *Primula vulgaris*, and *Primula vulgaris* 'Elizabeth Dickey'

The primrose is a familiar plant which inhabits woodland glades and hedge banks, as well as open grassland that has not been ploughed or cultivated. The primrose has produced a motley assortment of mutants, some ornamental, some ugly. Examples are the jack-in-the-green primrose with an enlarged green calyx, and the double primrose with a proliferation of petals. Elizabeth Dickey gathered hers unwittingly in a hedge bank near Ballymoney, County Antrim.

Primula vulgaris (right and detail)
Primula vulgaris 'Elizabeth Dickey' (left)

SLIEVE DONARD
NURSERY

I remember that when I was a boy I spent a few shillings on some plants that I had selected from the catalogue of the Slieve Donard Nursery of Newcastle, County Down. I had my own small patch of garden, and it was thrilling to receive the parcel containing the little plants. I recall that they were very carefully and skilfully wrapped in straw and made up into a tight bundle. The plants were probably not the most suitable ones for the north-facing bed of dense clay, and they struggled.

'The Donard', as it was familiarly called, had been established by Thomas Ryan (1879–1921) in 1904. In 1912 James Coey (1863–1921) acquired the lease and soon afterwards engaged William Slinger (1878–1961) to run the nursery. Slinger took full control in 1922. Willie Slinger's main interests were roses and daffodils. After 1946 his eldest son Leslie (1907–1974), a 'shrub man', was in charge and oversaw the nursery's rise to brilliance and international prominence. 'The Donard' closed in 1975 shortly after Leslie Slinger's unexpected death.

It was not easy to choose the plants to illustrate the excellence of this one nursery, as there were so many candidates. *Forsythia* 'Lynwood Variety' was a 'sport', a 'small branch which had gone wrong', found by Miss Nora Adair in 1933. *Mahonia* 'Charity', 'one of the finest shrubs ever raised', was selected from a batch of Donard-raised seedlings that had been sold to the Surrey nurseryman John Russell. Several of these ended up in the Savill Gardens at Windsor, where 'Charity' was named. *Rhododendron* 'Evelyn Slinger' was one of the last plants introduced by the nursery, and one of a group of rhododendrons that were deliberately bred there.

37

Forsythia × *intermedia* 'Lynwood Variety'

A bargain: the Slieve Donard Nursery gave Miss Adare of Lynwood, Cookstown, County Tyrone, some daffodil bulbs in exchange for the original cuttings of this award-winning *Forsythia*. 'Lynwood Variety' has large, bright flowers and is a hardy, reliable deciduous shrub.

Mahonia × media 'Charity'

There is a double Irish connection in 'Charity'. *Mahonia* commemorates the Irish-American horticulturist Bernard McMahon (*c.* 1775–1816) of Philadelphia.

This excellent winter-blooming evergreen shrub was an accidental seedling raised at the Slieve Donard Nursery. 'Charity' was selected and named by Sir Eric Savill.

Rhododendron 'Evelyn Slinger'

'Evelyn Slinger' is unusual in having a frilly, coloured calyx around the base of the corolla, similar in texture and colour to the corolla. This cultivar has the dwarf hardy Japanese species *Rhododendron yakusimanum* in its lineage, and was named after one of Ruby and Leslie Slinger's daughters, now Mrs Evelyn Deane.

ROWALLANE'S FINDLINGS

Hugh Armytage-Moore (1873–1954) inherited Rowallane, an estate situated a short distance from the centre of Saintfield in County Down, from his uncle, the Reverend John Moore, in 1903. He soon set about establishing, with the assistance of his highly accomplished head gardener, William Watson, an outstanding collection of hardy trees and shrubs for which the garden is renowned. Today Rowallane is owned by the National Trust and is open to the public.

There are many memorable plants growing in Rowallane: a fine handkerchief tree, billowing clumps of rhododendrons, wild orchids in the grassy areas. There are also excellent plants named after the garden, which are widely available. There were close connections between Rowallane and the Slieve Donard Nursery, which was responsible for marketing some of the best, including the quince, St John's-wort and candelabra primrose that Wendy Walsh painted. As well as these three, mention may be made of the fine *Crocosmia masoniorum* 'Rowallane Yellow', *Viburnum plicatum* 'Rowallane' (the original shrub survives in the walled garden), several lily-of-the-valley bushes – *Pieris formosa* var. *forrestii* 'Rowallane', *Pieris* 'Rowallane Pearl' – and the diminutive *Rhododendron hanceanum* 'Rowallane'.

What was Rowallane's secret? Undoubtedly the owner, and his attention to detail and skill as a horticulturist. After a four-day visit in the spring of 1942, Lady Moore wrote in appreciation: 'You cultivate so well. Your seedlings always seem to grow – do you ever have a failure, or a box of miffs? Another very delightful thing for us in going about your garden, is your close touch with your plants, your everyday companionship. This has come from so many having been grown by you for seed.'

Chaenomeles × superba 'Rowallane Seedling'

The original shrub of this early-flowering ornamental quince, which was a chance seedling in the early 1900s, still grows in the outer walled garden at Rowallane.

A hardy, deciduous, spreading shrub, this is a magnificent plant, ideal for planting on a low bank or against a sunny wall.

Hypericum 'Rowallane Hybrid'

There are few St John's-worts to match this one. It is capable of forming a shrub at least two metres tall which will be covered with flowers throughout the summer. Like many other garden plants, this one arose by chance, as a seedling, in Rowallane.

Primula 'Rowallane Rose'

Candelabra primroses have their origins in the Far East, whence several species were introduced in the early twentieth century. When grown together they hybridized, and some garden-worthy variants were noticed among the resulting seedlings. 'Rowallane Rose' is not fertile, so it has to be propagated by division, which is best done immediately after flowering.

GLASNEVIN

CONNECTIONS

The National Botanic Gardens, Glasnevin, has existed for more than two centuries and during that time hundreds of thousands of plants must have flourished there. As other portraits in this collection indicate, Glasnevin has acted as a horticultural and botanical hub, raising new plants from every continent and then distributing these to other gardens in Ireland and elsewhere.

In many instances the exact histories of the plants have not been recorded and we can only guess what may have been their original sources. For example, the history of the tree rhododendron named 'Fernhill Silver' is merely an anecdote. David Moore, it is said, gave the rhododendron to Mr and Mrs Edmund Darley who lived at Fernhill – but the story cannot be verified in the Gardens' archives. It is also said that the shrub was raised from seeds collected by Joseph Hooker, son of the director of the Royal Botanic Gardens, Kew; some packets of young Hooker's Sikkimese rhododendron seeds were donated to Glasnevin in 1850.

Much less is known about the potato vine which bears the Gardens' name. As early as the 1880s, a superior form of *Solanum crispum*, a native of South America, was recorded at the Glasnevin Botanic Gardens and it was probably this plant that was distributed in the early 1900s.

Between about 1907 and 1915, Charles Frederick Ball conducted a breeding programme at Glasnevin, aiming to raise new garden-worthy plants. He had several enduring successes with *Escallonia*, and also worked with *Mahonia*, *Ribes* and *Berberis*, although none of these survive. Coerced, by being sent white feathers, into enlisting in the Royal Dublin Fusiliers, Ball died from shrapnel wounds at Gallipoli during the disastrous Dardanelles Campaign. The exceptional *Escallonia* 'C. F. Ball' commemorates this tragic plantsman.

Escallonia rubra 'C. F. Ball'

Charles Frederick Ball (1879–1915), assistant keeper at the Glasnevin Botanic Gardens, was among the many men killed during the First World War.

He had raised several new varieties of *Escallonia* – one he named after his wife, 'Alice'. 'C. F. Ball' is an outstanding hardy evergreen shrub.

Rhododendron arboreum 'Fernhill Silver'

The watercolour of this lovely variety of the archetypal tree rhododendron was the first painting in the *Florilegium* series. Mature plants exist in the gardens at Fernhill, Sandyford, County Dublin, and at Mount Usher, County Wicklow. According to tradition, this rhododendron was raised at and distributed from the Glasnevin Botanic Gardens in the mid-1800s. In *An Irish Florilegium*, this shrub was given the name 'Fernhill', but that was not permissible because another rhododendron already bore the name. 'Fernhill Silver', alluding to the silvery underside of the leaves, was registered as the replacement.

Solanum crispum 'Glasnevin'

The history of this potato vine is not known. Plants of a distinct, but unnamed variety were distributed from the Glasnevin Botanic Gardens in 1901. Five years later, 'Glasnevin *Solanum crispum*' was noted for the first time in the Gardens' distribution records. It is an undemanding, vigorous semi-evergreen shrub, which does well when trained against a wall.

FROM GREAT GARDENS

Irish gardens, large and small, contain a very diverse assembly of plants, some simply species transplanted from the wild, but many others are cultivars. When rich collections are well maintained, there is great scope for new plants to come about by chance.

Mount Usher, at Ashford in County Wicklow, is famous as a garden that follows the principles of the renowned Irish horticulturist William Robinson (1838–1935) who advocated informal natural arrangements of hardy plants, and there are many rare and unusual species in the collections, especially from the southern hemisphere. Although both *Eucryphia glutinosa* and *Eucryphia cordifolia* come from Chile, they do not co-exist in the wild. When growing in close proximity in gardens, they have accidentally crossed, producing the fine *Eucryphia × nymansensis*. This was first noticed at Nymans in Sussex, England, and the same cross occurred at Mount Usher.

Nymans was the family home of Anne, Countess of Rosse (1902–1992). After their marriage, Lord and Lady Rosse set about expanding the plant collection in the demesne at Birr Castle, the Rosse family seat, in County Offaly. It is believed that two different tree peonies, the yellow-flowered *Paeonia lutea* var. *ludlowii* and the deep mahogany-red *Paeonia delavayi* accidentally hybridized at Birr to yield a shrub with large yellow flowers streaked with red – the original plant of 'Anne Rosse' is still alive.

Mulroy House and Glenveagh Castle are situated in the north of County Donegal. The fifth Earl of Leitrim (1879–1952) and his second wife, Anne (1893–1984), were passionate about rhododendrons and magnolias and assembled an excellent collection, which was virtually obliterated by Hurricane Debbie in 1961. Some hybrid rhododendrons raised by Lord Leitrim were purchased by Henry Plumer McIlhenny (1910–1986) for Glenveagh Castle, where there is another remarkable garden full of interesting and rare plants. One of the Mulroy seedlings was subsequently selected by Mary Forrest for naming; because it was a seedling from 'Vanguard', a hybrid raised at Headfort House (see p. 198), the name registered was 'Mulroy Vanguard'.

Eucryphia × *nymansensis* 'Mount Usher'

Mount Usher at Ashford in County Wicklow is one of Ireland's finest gardens, with a long history of sheltering plants of somewhat tender disposition.

This evergreen was a chance hybrid seedling which arose there, and the original plant, now a massive tree, still grows in the garden.

Paeonia 'Anne Rosse'

Among the wild species of tree peonies introduced from China during the twentieth century were two contrasting kinds: some had pure yellow flowers, whereas others had deep mahogany-red blossoms. The red flushing and stamens in 'Anne Rosse', raised at Birr Castle, County Offaly, suggest that it came about because a yellow- and a red-flowered tree peony crossed, but similar plants are now known in the wild in China.

Rhododendron 'Mulroy Vanguard'

A small shrub nursery operated at Mulroy House, County Donegal, during the 1940s and early 1950s, selling especially rhododendrons. This cultivar was among seedlings listed in the 1950 catalogue as "New Hybrid ('Vanguard' × Thomsonii Grandiflorum)". 'Mulroy Vanguard' was selected at Glenveagh Castle and named in 1986.

THE NAMES
OF PLACES

Ballawley, Straffan, Grallagh: names of places and names for flowers.

Straffan House in County Kildare had a famous garden when the Bartons lived there. In the early 1900s Frederick Burbidge would cycle the fifteen miles from Ballsbridge to Straffan, by way of the Strawberry Beds and Lucan, just to see the snowdrops. In season, 'clouds' of them floated on the lawns. Snowdrops are the quintessential winter flower but there is no native *Galanthus* species. 'Straffan' and 'Hill Poë' are just two of the numerous snowdrop cultivars which have originated in Ireland's gardens.

Captain James Hill Poë's daughter Blanche (1876–1968) made her own garden at Grallagh, Nenagh, County Tipperary. Around 1940 she found some seedlings of the bright-yellow-blossomed *Anthemis* which were different, and wisely she propagated them. One was to be named 'Grallagh Glory' and the other 'Grallagh Gold'.

Ballawley will be a more familiar name, for there are several plants that were called after the place, including a dark-red-flowered mossy saxifrage, and a widely grown and highly recommended *Bergenia*. Situated in the foothills of the Dublin Mountains in Dundrum, Ballawley Park was the home of the Shaw-Smiths and contained a fine rock garden stocked with interesting plants. Ballawley Alpine Nursery was established to sell surplus plants, but soon was also introducing new ones including several good *Aubrieta* and *Dianthus* cultivars.

49

Galanthus 'Hill Poë' and 'Straffan'

Around 1900, a 'double' snowdrop was found growing under a walnut tree at Riverston, Nenagh, County Tipperary, by Captain James Hill Poë (1845–1930). It was considered the best of its kind, for 'double' snowdrops often have ugly, misshapen flowers due to the proliferation of petals. 'Straffan', the loveliest and most famous of Irish snowdrops, was also a foundling, first noticed in the garden of Straffan House, County Kildare, during the late 1870s. Strong bulbs will often produce two flowers, thus extending the flowering season. Like all named snowdrops, 'Hill Poë' and 'Straffan' can only be increased by division.

Galanthus 'Hill Poë' (right)
Galanthus 'Straffan' (left)

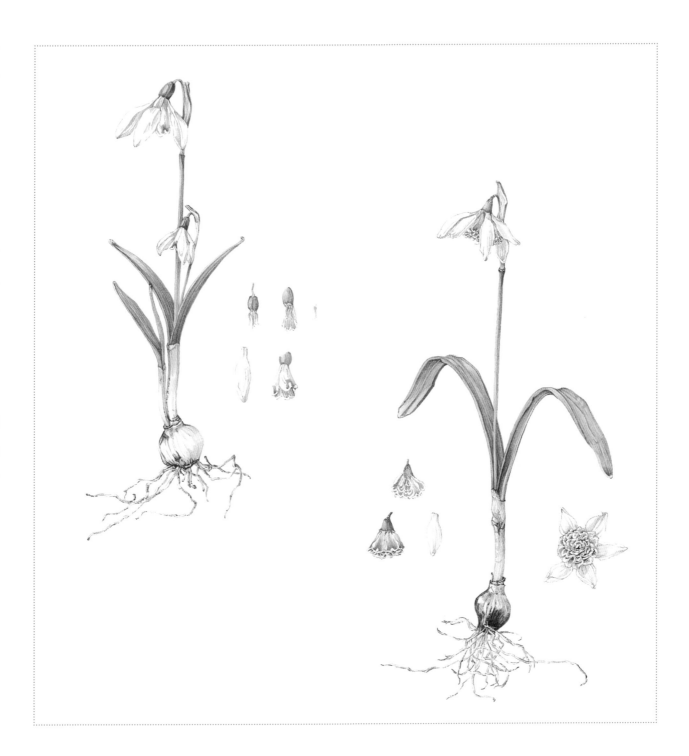

50

Anthemis 'Grallagh Gold'

This outstanding daisy arose as a chance seedling in Blanche Poë's garden at Grallagh, Nenagh, County Tipperary.

'Grallagh Gold' is a short-lived perennial, which needs to be propagated by cuttings at least every other year.

57

Bergenia 'Ballawley'

Early-flowering perennials are a boon to gardeners. The cabbage-like foliage of this outstanding hybrid takes on crimson tints in winter. The young leaves are plain, glossy green and so provide an excellent foil for the magenta flowers. *Bergenia* 'Ballawley' originated at Ballawley Park, Dundrum, County Dublin; it was introduced in 1944.

VARIOUS
VARIEGATIONS

Gardeners are restless spirits, it seems, not satisfied unless they have something new and something different to cultivate. They are always on the lookout for novel plants, and for some enthusiastic gardeners plants which have variegated foliage provide the greatest novelty. Others dislike variegation, dismissing plants with mottled leaves as abominable aberrations unworthy of cultivation.

Evergreen shrubs that possess variegated leaves can be valuable in providing contrasting shades and tones in the garden, and they were especially cherished by nineteenth-century gardeners who followed the fashion for dense evergreen shrubberies. In the winter, variegated foliage provides a splash of brightness among darkening sombre greens.

The manner of variegation differs not just from species to species, but also from individual leaf to individual leaf – no two leaves on a variegated plant will have exactly the same pattern of mottles, streaks or patches. This is very obvious in larger-leaved shrubs such as the hollies. It is this intrinsic diversity which can make a variegated plant more charming than one of a uniform colour – green leaves flecked with red, cream and white are more attractive than the bilious yellow-greens of some so-called 'golden' plants.

Variegation has no natural advantages. In fact, plants with variegated foliage are likely to be less robust than their all-green counterparts. So wild plants which are naturally variegated are relatively few and far between.

Irish gardens have produced around sixty variegated cultivars in about forty genera, ranging in stature from a giant redwood and a sycamore to several primroses and tutsans. The most prolific has been *Pittosporum* – 'Silver Queen' (Pl. 72) being the first.

52

Azara microphylla 'Variegata'

The eccentric Cork plantsman William Edward Gumbleton (1840–1911) had an exceptional garden at Belgrove, near Cobh (formerly Queenstown). He was quite a 'magpie', collecting all sorts of unusual shrubs, herbaceous perennials, bulbs and annuals. Belgrove was the original source of this slightly frost-tender evergreen shrub, which has tiny and inconspicuous yet sweetly scented flowers.

53

Ilex × altaclerensis 'Hendersonii' and 'Lawsoniana'

The plain holly, named 'Hendersonii', was raised at Dunganstown, County Wexford, during the early nineteenth century, in the Hodgins family's nursery. 'Lawsoniana' was a 'sport' on 'Hendersonii', which occurred in the same family's nursery at Cloughjordan, County Tipperary, later that century. Both hollies are female and bear berries, and they are robust, hardy shrubs.

Ilex × altaclerensis 'Hendersonii' (upper)
Ilex × altaclerensis 'Lawsoniana' (lower)

54

Luma apiculata 'Glanleam Gold'

Some variegated plants arise as seedlings. A variegated seedling of the South American myrtle (formerly named *Myrtus apiculata*) was noticed by Neil Treseder (1913–1996), a Cornish nurseryman from Truro, in the garden at Glanleam on Valentia Island, County Kerry, then owned by Lieutenant Colonel Richard John Uniacke (1909–1989). The seedling developed into a fine garden plant. The original tree, now more than five metres tall, survives in Glanleam.

PLANT BREEDING

Breeding new plants by raising them from seed takes an enormous amount of patience. There are no instant results. Years may pass before the seedlings are large enough to produce their first flowers, and often these turn out to be disappointing, no better than the parents, or, worse, much inferior.

In the annals of Irish horticulture Alice Louisa Lawrenson (d. 1900) has primacy as the first women known to have carried out any deliberate breeding of plants. She patiently and carefully selected for bright colours and flowers with extra petals, thereby creating a lineage of crown anemones, which still is widely grown.

Like Mrs Lawrenson, Miss Doris Findlater (1895–1981) was an amateur, in the sense of not being a professional horticulturist or botanist. She chose to work with Guernsey lilies, *Nerine*, and was very successful, producing some exceptional bulbs. It required a lot more patience to raise a new *Nerine* than to raise a new crown anemone, and Miss Findlater's bulbs have never been widely grown.

Daffodil seedlings, like those of Guernsey lilies, take four or more years to reach flowering stage. Many more years will elapse before a daffodil can be bulked up, named and released. For example, the daffodil named 'Wendy Walsh' was a seedling produced from a seed-pod that had formed in 1976 after Kate Reade had deliberately cross-pollinated two of her own earlier seedlings. The new seeds were sown, and then the waiting began. What would the seedlings be like? Anything could have happened!

55

Anemone coronaria 'St Bridgid'

Mrs Alice Lawrenson of Howth, who used the nom-de-plume 'St Bridgid', was an expert gardener, and by dint of careful selection she created the St Bridgid group of the crown anemone during the late 1800s. She grew her crown anemones from seeds gathered from selected plants.

Nerine 'Glensavage Gem' and 'John Fanning'

The petals of 'Glensavage Gem' sparkle in certain lights as if spattered with golden dust. When the claret-rose flowers of 'John Fanning' are mature, they acquire a distinctive purplish tinge.

These two Guernsey lilies were among numerous seedlings raised by Miss Doris Findlater of Glensavage, Glenageary, County Dublin.

Nerine 'Glensavage Gem' (upper centre)
Nerine 'John Fanning' (lower left and right)

57

Narcissus 'Wendy Walsh'

'Wendy Walsh', registered in 1988, came from 'Tynan' crossed with an unnamed seedling. All three were raised at Carncairn Lodge, Broughshane, County Antrim, by Mrs Kate Reade, who retired recently as a professional breeder of daffodils. Her legacy of fine bulbs, also including 'Foundling' (Pl. 59), will continue to enthral plantsmen for decades to come. This watercolour was originally published in *A Prospect of Irish Flowers* (1990).

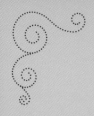

IRISH DAFFODILS

A passion for daffodils is an incurable affliction, nicknamed 'Yellow Fever'. For more than a century and a quarter, Ireland has had a coterie of sufferers from that weakness, and a remarkable daffodil industry producing new cultivars and supplying these to gardeners throughout the world. In 1883 the inimitable and impulsive Cork nurseryman William Baylor Hartland (1836–1912) issued his first catalogue and three years later published his whimsically titled *Ye Original Little Book of Daffodils*. Hartland was encouraged by Frederick Burbidge (see *Calceolaria × burbidgei*, Pl. 62) of the Trinity College Botanic Garden, Ballsbridge, and in turn Hartland stimulated the Antrim plantsman Guy Livingstone Wilson (1885–1962) to take up the breeding of new daffodils.

Wilson, like Hartland, had a special delight in white-flowered daffodils, and he chose evocative names for them – 'Driven Snow', 'Everest', 'Kanchenjunga'. He was also interested in bicoloured flowers, in which there was a distinct contrast in the colours of the corona ('trumpet') and the petals. Guy Wilson raised and named more than six hundred daffodils, and not a few remain in cultivation.

There were many other Irish daffodil-breeders. Joseph Lionel Richardson (1890–1961) and his wife Helen (1903–1978) were probably the most prolific, with at least eight hundred named cultivars to their credit. I particularly like the wonderful pink-trumpeted 'Salmon Trout', which was produced before 1948, but 'Kingscourt' is one of the most enduring of their excellent yellow flowers.

Guy Wilson lived at Broughshane in County Antrim, and by coincidence that village is also where Kate Reade lives. It was a pleasure to visit Carncairn and discuss daffodils with Kate and to hear the stories of some of her bulbs. When I suggested to Kate that it would be a nice idea to name a daffodil after Wendy, she agreed with alacrity and we chose the one which has been selected for the frontispiece of this book.

58

Narcissus 'Cantatrice'

Among Guy Wilson's white daffodils 'Cantatrice' was exceptional, the flower having 'a beautiful pure white trumpet of smoothest texture'. It first bloomed in 1932, received an award of merit in 1939, and continued heading the prize lists for more than thirty years.

59

Narcissus 'Foundling'

When Wendy Walsh painted Kate Reade's 'Foundling' in 1986 it was possible to write that this diminutive daffodil had won more prizes than any other daffodil. It was an orphan seedling, of unknown parentage, yet it has continued to prove its excellence. 'Foundling' deserves a place in every garden.

Narcissus 'Kingscourt'

Lionel Richardson believed this daffodil, with flowers of 'faultless form' and 'superb quality', was 'the finest exhibition yellow trumpet seen'. It held prime place among exhibition daffodils between 1948 and 1963, and currently holds the Royal Horticultural Society's Award of Garden Merit, given to outstanding, reliable and readily available plants.

DELIBERATELY
RAISED HYBRIDS

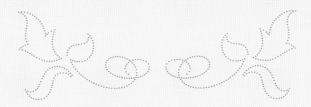

In the eighteenth century, botanists and gardeners learned that by transferring pollen from the stamens (the male parts) of one flower on to the stigma (the female part) of another flower belonging to a different species, a hybrid (a 'cross') may be produced. In the nineteenth century, this technique was exploited more and more to provide novel plants for gardens.

At Glasnevin Botanic Gardens, William Pope (1834–1915) cross-pollinated species of the American pitcherplants (*Sarracenia*, Pl. 29) to produce a pioneering series of hybrids. New daffodil hybrids were also being raised in Glasnevin around the same time. At the Trinity College Botanic Garden in Ballsbridge, Frederick William Burbidge (1847–1905) crossed different species of slipperwort (*Calceolaria*) creating the hybrid which was named after him. The College slipperwort had to be propagated by cuttings, and was still grown by the College gardeners into the 1990s.

At Cork about 1880, in his private garden, Lakelands, where he had a large, heated glasshouse, William Horatio Crawford (1811–1888) crossed different species of the genus *Brownea*, most of which are enormous rainforest trees. To grow these tropical species successfully and to get them to produce flowers and seeds were remarkable achievements for a private garden in temperate latitudes. Crawford went further and created several hybrids including the sumptuous, eponymous *Brownea* × *crawfordii*.

These are only two examples of inter-species hybrids raised deliberately in Ireland in the past two centuries. The same techniques are used by daffodil and rose breeders although the parent plants, in these cases, are usually selected cultivars rather than species.

New techniques are now employed in plant breeding. Scientists can manipulate plants in ways undreamt of by the hybridizers of old. For example, a virus-like agent which causes streaking of the petals in *Pelargonium* ('indoor geranium') can be used to induce variegated flowers. 'Koko' was created in this way by Judy Cassells working in the Department of Plant Science at University College, Cork.

Brownea × *crawfordii*

Brownea, named after Dr Patrick Browne
(*c.* 1720–1790) of County Mayo, is a
genus of trees native in tropical America.
They are fast-growing plants which in
Ireland and other temperate regions
must be protected in a heated glasshouse.
Crawford bequeathed his *Brownea* hybrids
to the Royal Botanic Gardens, Kew, where
Brownea × *crawfordii* still is grown.

Calceolaria × burbidgei

This hybrid was created at the Trinity College Botanic Garden, Ballsbridge, during the late 1800s, and it is named after the garden's curator Frederick Burbidge. Another watercolour of the College slipperwort by Wendy Walsh was featured on an Irish postage stamp issued in 1987 to mark the tercentenary of the first of the University of Dublin's botanic gardens.

Pelargonium 'Koko'

We usually think of viruses as causes of human and animal illnesses and plant diseases, but sometimes they are relatively harmless. In the 1970s, one was discovered which produces attractive variegation in the petals of 'indoor geraniums' (*Pelargonium*), and this petal-streak agent was used in 1984 to transform 'Rio Grande' into 'Koko'.

ROSE-BORDERED HEM

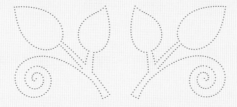

Ireland and roses are inseparable. *Roisin dubh*, the little black rose, 'my dark Rosaleen', was a metaphor for Ireland in the sixteenth century. We know roses were deliberately cultivated in Irish gardens as early as the late 1500s, for the deeds of Trinity College, Dublin, record them. Later Thomas Moore penned an immortal lyric poem about the last rose of summer; the actual rose which inspired him was almost certainly the pink-blossomed China rose that is still grown under the name 'Old Blush'.

Wendy Walsh has painted numerous roses, including the native hybrid *Rosa* × *hibernica* (Pl. 31), and the exotic Macartney's rose, which exemplifies her pleasure and consummate skill in painting white flowers on white paper. These are wild plants transplanted into gardens, not man-made cultivars.

The breeding of roses, like the breeding of daffodils, has been a special facet of horticulture in the north of Ireland since the second half of the nineteenth century and continues so to this day. The rose dynasties of Ulster are famous: the Dicksons and the McGredys. We chose 'Irish Elegance' to represent deliberate rose-breeding because it is a rare and significant plant.

Yet not all cultivars are deliberately produced; sometimes they come about by chance. 'Souvenir de St Anne's', for example, was a 'sport' on the old double-blossomed Bourbon rose 'Souvenir de La Malmaison'. This charming rose was not widely distributed because Olivia Guinness, Baroness Ardilaun of Ashford (1850–1925), in whose Dublin garden it had arisen, made those to whom she gave cuttings promise never to let anyone else have it. Fortunately this prohibition lapsed or was ignored.

Rosa 'Irish Elegance'

Single-flowered hybrid tea roses are no longer fashionable, so cultivars like 'Irish Elegance' have all but vanished. We eventually found a plant at Fernhill, Sandyford, County Dublin. 'Irish Elegance' was one of a series of similar free-flowering, vigorous, hardy roses, 'gems of the first water', raised by Dicksons of Hawlmark, Newtownards, County Down, and released in the early 1900s.

Rosa 'Souvenir de St Anne's'

About 1910, at St Anne's, Clontarf, County Dublin, a shrub of 'Souvenir de La Malmaison' produced a shoot bearing pale pink, semi-double flowers, different from the usual blossoms of this rose. The 'sport' was noticed by the head gardener, Andrew Campbell (1852–1917), who propagated it. This rose is superb, long-flowering, disease-resistant and fragrant.

Rosa bracteata

Macartney's rose was brought as seed from China when an embassy which had been sent by King George III to the Qianlong Emperor returned to England in 1794. The Ambassador and Minister Plenipotentiary was Earl Macartney (1737–1806) of Lisanoure, County Antrim. This species is late-flowering, lemon-scented, very thorny and semi-evergreen, but not fully hardy.

SCOTTISH LINKS

There are numerous connections of different kinds between Irish gardens and Scotland. In the eighteenth and nineteenth centuries, many of the professional plantsmen who were appointed to senior positions in Irish gardens were of Scottish birth and training. This is exemplified by the botanical gardens in Cork and Belfast, as well as the Trinity College Botanic Garden and Glasnevin Botanic Gardens in Dublin; they all had Scotsmen as curators or head gardeners. These men were not just brilliant gardeners – they were also excellent field botanists and plant hunters. James Townsend Mackay (see *Mackaya bella*, Pl. 92) and David Moore (see p. 213, and *Crinum moorei*, Pl. 77) were among this company of botanical Scotsmen.

John Scouler (1804–1871), a native of Glasgow, was not a gardener. He was engaged as a ship's surgeon in 1824, and so became the companion of David Douglas, a fellow Scot, on a voyage to the north-west of America by way of Cape Horn. Scouler collected plants and several were named after him. A few years after his return, he became Professor of Mineralogy to the Royal Dublin Society and moved to Dublin.

Two of these plants illustrate another kind of link with Scotland. Mrs Frazer (Vera) Mackie (d. 1979), whose garden, Guincho, at Helen's Bay, County Down, contained many rare plants, found the purple-leaved elder in a Scottish hedgerow, took some cuttings and propagated it. It grew at Guincho for some time before it was noticed by Sir Harold Hillier, whose famous English nursery named the elder and introduced it commercially.

The story of the blue Himalayan poppy is more complicated. Alexander Ormiston Curle (1866–1955), an eminent Scottish archaeologist and museum director, raised it and passed offsets to his friends. The poppy reached Ireland and was obtained by the Slieve Donard Nursery on whose show stands it was to feature regularly. Eventually, needing a name, the poppy was called after the nursery, which in turn took its name from the highest peak of the Mourne Mountains in County Down.

Meconopsis × *sheldonii* 'Slieve Donard'

This famous perennial Himalayan poppy had a complicated career before being named. Because the poppy is a sterile hybrid, it is can only be propagated by division, best done immediately after the flowers fade. It needs a rich, friable loam enriched with leaf-mould, and it prefers a moist, cool situation.

Penstemon fruticosus var. *scouleri* 'Alba'

The white-flowered cultivar of the littleleaf bush penstemon is a perennial subshrub. The parental variety comes from the north-western United States and western Canada. Its name commemorates John Scouler, who collected specimens in that region during 1825. *Penstemon fruticosus* is an ideal plant for a rockery or trough.

Purple-leaved elder, *Sambucus nigra* f. *porphyrophylla* 'Guincho Purple'

Elders with dark purple foliage are now familiar garden plants, yet when 'Guincho Purple' was introduced commercially in the early 1970s, it was the only one of its kind. Vera Mackie found this elder in Scotland about 1957.

ANTIPODEAN PLANTS

The first plants from New Zealand to come into cultivation in Europe arrived in 1771 when Captain James Cook and his companions returned to England after observing the transit of Venus in Tahiti. During the voyage, HMS *Endeavour* circumnavigated New Zealand and the entire coastline was charted.

In the first half of the nineteenth century, as more New Zealand plants arrived, Irish gardeners learned, by trial and loss, that some would thrive when planted outdoors, and today such plants as the cabbage palm, *Cordyline australis*, and the hedging shrub *Griselinia littoralis* are ubiquitous in our gardens. Indeed, quite a number of New Zealand plants provide excellent evergreens for use as hedges in coastal gardens.

An old familiar is *Pittosporum tenuifolium*, represented here by the variegated cultivar 'Silver Queen', which was one of the first new plants introduced by the Slieve Donard Nursery (see p. 109). The dark flowers are beautifully fragrant.

Other plants of New Zealand origin among the *Florilegium* paintings are a shrubby speedwell named after Geoffrey Taylour, fourth Marquis of Headfort (1878–1943), who was an expert plantsman with a particular interest in rhododendrons, which he raised from wild-collected seed, and conifers.

The third subject, Henry Travers's daisy-bush, was among a consignment of native plants from the Chatham Islands which Henry Hammersley Travers (1844–1928), a barrister turned professional plant collector, sent to the Glasnevin Botanic Gardens in 1908.

Hebe 'Headfortii'

The shrubby speedwells – formerly *Veronica* but now familiar by the name *Hebe* – are almost all native to New Zealand, and this one must have originated there. However, it is not a species known in the wild. A slightly tender shrub that thrives in sheltered, mild gardens, 'Headfortii' was raised at Headfort House, Kells, County Meath, before 1930.

Olearia 'Henry Travers'

The Chatham Islands are a remote archipelago to the east of New Zealand in the southern Pacific Ocean. Among the plants found there is this daisy-bush, which appears to be of hybrid origin.

Henry Travers, whose family had roots in County Limerick, introduced this shrub to Irish gardens. It needs protection from frost, and is another ideal shrub for coastal gardens.

Pittosporum tenuifolium 'Silver Queen'

This familiar evergreen shrub arose, as a 'sport', before 1914, probably in the garden of Castlewellan Castle, County Down. In May 1914, when shown in London, 'Silver Queen' was given the Royal Horticultural Society's prestigious Award of Merit, and it retains the RHS Award of Garden Merit.

WINTER GARDEN

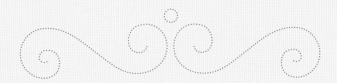

Present-day gardeners are spoilt for choice when they come to chose plants for an out-of-doors winter garden. A century and more ago there were comparatively few winter-flowering perennials, shrubs or trees available in Ireland. Mid-nineteenth-century winter gardens contained mainly evergreen shrubs; dark foliage was contrasted with variegated or golden. New plants arrived, and by the late 1800s correspondents to the gardening periodicals of the day would vie with each other to produce the longest lists of plants in bloom on Christmas Day or New Year's Day. Gradually, winter gardens were stocked with these plants. Winter-blossoming trees, shrubs and perennials became fashionable.

The tassel-bush was known to nineteenth-century gardeners – David Douglas, John Scouler's companion (see p. 189), had introduced it in the late 1820s. The male plants have attractive catkins, although these are not especially colourful, a subtle silvery grey-green with hints of gold. The hybrid unwittingly raised at Malahide Castle, County Dublin, in the 1960s has brighter, green and red catkins.

There is no native witch-hazel (*Hamamelis*) – these shrubs are only indigenous to eastern North America and the Far East. The witch-hazels are not related to the native hazel (*Corylus*), although the foliage looks similar. The finest witch-hazel, with brilliant yellow flowers, is the Chinese species *Hamamelis mollis*. There are now many different witch-hazels in cultivation, with petals which range from creamy yellow to vivid orange.

In mild years, the October cherry does not abide by its name and continues to produce flowers in mid-winter. The tree is deciduous and as the leaves fall, the small, semi-double pink flowers sprout from the bare twigs. Tom Smith (1840–1919) imported the tree from Japan, and it is just one of the thousands of plants which justified his claim that the Daisy Hill Nursery, which he owned, was 'the most interesting nursery probably in the world'. It certainly was a plantsman's treasure-house during the first few decades of the twentieth century.

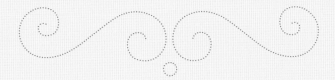

Hamamelis mollis

Chinese witch-hazel is now a familiar winter-flowering shrub. Dr Augustine Henry (see p. 229) provided the pressed, dried specimen from which the species was named and described in the late 1880s, but he did not collect seeds. In fact, this species was already growing in England in 1879, before Dr Henry travelled to China.

Prunus subhirtella 'Autumnalis'

Few small trees can compare with the October cherry, which blossoms in late autumn and again in early spring. Ours was in full flower as I wrote this on St Stephen's Day in 2007, and again had a sprinkling of blooms on St Patrick's Day in 2008. The October cherry was introduced to Irish gardeners in 1901 through the Daisy Hill Nursery, Newry, County Down.

Garrya × issaquahensis and Garrya × issaquahensis 'Pat Ballard'

This hybrid tassel-bush was raised from a packet of seeds received by Milo Talbot, Baron Talbot de Malahide (1912–1973) from Mrs Pat Ballard of Issaquah, Seattle, USA. The best of the male seedlings, with well-coloured catkins, was named after Mrs Ballard. Female plants have stiff, short catkins and produce grape-like clusters of fruits.

Garrya × issaquahensis female (lower left) and fruits (lower centre)
Garrya × issaquahensis 'Pat Ballard' (upper centre)

A DYNASTY
OF MOORES

David Moore, a 20-year-old trained gardener, came to Dublin in 1828 to work in the Trinity College Botanic Garden at Ballsbridge, Dublin. He was, like the curator James Townsend Mackay, a Scot. In 1834, Moore joined the Ordnance Survey and worked in the north of Ireland recording native plants.

Four years later, David Moore was appointed curator of the Royal Dublin Society's Botanic Gardens, Glasnevin, and remained in charge there until his death on 6 June 1879. Those four decades saw a dramatic increase in the diversity and number of plants grown in the Gardens, and a few of the new species were named after David Moore – probably the most handsome being the Natal lily, *Crinum moorei*.

David Moore first married in 1836 but both his first wife, Hannah, and his second wife, Isabella, died a few years after their respective marriages. Sir Frederick William Moore was the eldest son of David and his third wife, Margaret. He followed his father into horticulture, and was appointed curator at Glasnevin a few weeks after his father died. Frederick Moore, who was knighted in 1911, had a passion for tropical orchids. He retired as keeper of the Royal Botanic Gardens, Glasnevin, in 1922.

In 1901 Frederick Moore married Wilhelmina Phylis Paul, daughter of Mr and Mrs Robert Paul of Drumcondra. Phylis Moore (1878–1976) was not a trained horticulturist or botanist, as far as we know, yet she learned rapidly and became a highly skilled gardener. On Frederick's retirement, the Moores moved to Willbrook House in Rathfarnham, County Dublin, where they established their own garden, stocked with the choicest plants. There are several excellent cultivars named after Lady Moore, including a variegated *Acanthus*, an iris, a flowering quince and a broom.

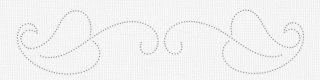

Coelogyne mooreana

Sir Frederick Moore VMH (1857–1949) assembled an unequalled collection of the smaller flowered species of tropical orchids at the Glasnevin Botanic Gardens during his keepership between 1879 and 1922. Several previously unknown orchid species were named in his honour, including this one which comes from Vietnam.

Crinum moorei

The Natal lily was among bulbs received at Glasnevin Botanic Gardens in 1862 from a Mr Webb. The lily first flowered there in 1869. Dr Joseph Hooker named it after Dr David Moore (1808–1879).

Moore's *Crinum* thrives in a sheltered, sunny spot, if utterly undisturbed. The progeny of the original introduction still grow at Glasnevin.

Cytisus 'Lady Moore' and 'Killiney Red'

Brooms with red flowers were a speciality of Watson's Nursery in Killiney, County Dublin, during the mid-1900s. Among the best were 'Lady Moore' and 'Killiney Red', which was described as the 'reddest broom'. The nursery closed in 1966. These shrubs have to be propagated by cuttings.

Cytisus 'Lady Moore' (centre)
Cytisus 'Killiney Red' (right)

MADDEN AND EDGEWORTH

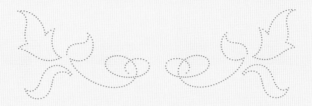

Edward Madden (1804–1857), whose family had links with Kilkenny and Waterford, and Michael Pakenham Edgeworth (1812–1881), born at Edgeworthstown, County Longford, had much in common, besides their Irish ancestry. They were both based in Bengal, India – Madden as a soldier and Edgeworth as a civil servant – during the 1840s. They knew one another, most probably because they shared a hobby – plant hunting in the Himalaya. They also were generous to the Glasnevin Botanic Gardens at this period, sending packets of seeds which they had gathered in the mountains. Madden also was to send bulbs and orchids.

Glasnevin's collections greatly benefited from the hundreds of packets of seeds that comprised Madden's collections in the decade up to 1850. Among the plants which were raised from these seeds was the giant Himalayan lily, *Cardiocrinum giganteum*, that is now a feature of numerous Irish gardens. Madden reported that in Kumaon the hollow flower-stems of the exhausted lily were used to make musical pipes.

Madden is commemorated in a number of plants: the genus *Maddenia* bears his name, as does a beautiful scented white rhododendron. As it so happens, *Rhododendron edgeworthii* also has flowers which are white but they do not have the scent of Madden's species.

Like Madden, Edgeworth is commemorated in a genus: *Edgeworthia* is a winter-blooming relative of *Daphne*, notable for its very flexible stems and yellow flowers.

Abelia triflora

Seed of this hardy, deciduous shrub or small tree, with highly fragrant flowers, was collected near Simla, India, during the late 1840s by Major Edward Madden, and seedlings first flowered at Glasnevin Botanic Gardens in 1852. *Abelia* is related to the honeysuckles.

Buddleja crispa

There are about a hundred different species of *Buddleja*, commonly called butterfly bushes. Seed of this hardy species was sent from India to Ireland by Major Edward Madden; a plant raised at Glasnevin Botanic Gardens blossomed in 1854. Michael Pakenham Edgeworth also gathered this *Buddleja*, for it is in a list of seeds received at Edgeworthstown during June 1841: the fate of those seeds is not recorded.

Primula edgeworthii

Michael Pakenham Edgeworth, one of the twenty-two children of the Reverend Richard Lovell Edgeworth, spent many years in India. In his spare time, he collected seeds and sent some to his half-sister, the novelist Maria Edgeworth, for her garden at Edgeworthstown. Several new plants, including this primrose, were named after him. It is a choice plant, but not an easy one to grow, requiring cold winters and shady, moist conditions. The little primrose may not be entitled to the name *Primula edgeworthii* – there is an opinion that it should be called *Primula nana*, which is an earlier name for an almost identical species, also from the Himalaya. If the two primroses are found to be the same, the earlier name has to be employed.

AUGUSTINE

HENRY

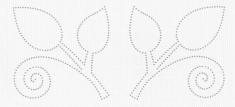

Augustine Henry was born on 2 July 1857 in Dundee, but that was a simple 'accident of birth'. His father, Bernard, was from the north of Ireland, so young 'Austin' was brought up at Tyanee on the west bank of the River Bann in County Londonderry. After attending Cookstown Academy he went to Queen's College, Galway, and studied natural history. Attracted to a career as a doctor in the Chinese Imperial Maritime Customs Service, Henry quickly acquired medical qualifications. For almost twenty years he was to work at various places in China.

Partly as his hobby and partly to assist in the identification of traditional medicinal products for the Customs returns, Henry began to collect, press and dry plant specimens. He contacted the Royal Botanic Gardens, Kew, seeking help in getting the samples identified. Thus began an interest in botany, which led to Dr Henry becoming one of the most famous plant collectors of the late nineteenth century.

Henry left China for the last time on the last day of the nineteenth century. He took up the study of trees, attended the French forestry school at Nancy, and eventually returned to Ireland becoming Professor of Forestry in University College, Dublin. Henry died in Dublin on 23 March 1930.

There are dozens of Chinese plants named after Augustine Henry, using either his Christian name or his surname. Among the species with names derived from Augustine are a rhododendron, a begonia and a St John's-wort. There was also *Henrya augustiniana*, a double eponym, but the species is now called *Tylophora augustiniana*. As for species named *henryi*, there are many, and the handsome lily is probably the most familiar.

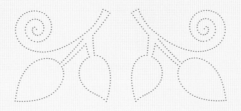

Davidia involucrata

The dove, or handkerchief, tree is a native of central China and has been cultivated in Ireland since about 1903. Dr Augustine Henry saw a tree in the wild and sent the first seeds to Europe, but they were pickled, so he did not introduce the tree into cultivation. However, the dove tree prompted Henry to promote the idea of a professional collector coming out to China to collect it.

Lilium henryi

Dr Henry discovered this lily in the river gorges near Yichang in central China. When he left Yichang he brought bulbs with him and some reached the Royal Botanic Gardens, Kew. Henry's lily is lime-tolerant and hardy, making it one of the easiest lilies to cultivate.

Rhododendron augustinii

Augustine Henry's rhododendron comes from central China. It was found near Patung, Hubei, by a native collector who was employed by Henry to gather and press specimens for Kew. This evergreen shrub is one of the few rhododendrons suitable for gardens with alkaline soil. The colour varies, some plants producing purer blue flowers than others.

CHINESE

COLLECTIONS

We have come to appreciate the personal links which Ireland and her gardens have with China. Of those links, the one which always come to the fore is that involving Dr Augustine Henry (see p. 229), and he is paramount among the Irish men and women who contributed to European knowledge of the riches of the flora of China. In terms of the number of pressed specimens collected, Henry far exceeds everyone else: more than 150,000 specimens are credited to him, but we know that he also employed native Chinese collectors, so the ones he gathered personally will not have been quite so numerous.

While he collected countless plants, Dr Henry did not introduce many into cultivation, as he did not have the time to spend collecting seeds. We have explicit records of only around thirty plants raised from seeds sent by him from China. These include the ornamental raspberry portrayed by Wendy Walsh, and a variant of the now familiar butterfly bush, *Buddleja davidii*. Henry also found the wild ancestor of the China rose, the true *Rosa chinensis*. Yet he was neither the first nor the last Irish collector to pocket a few seeds while visiting China.

Thomas Watters (*c*. 1840–1904), who served as British Consul in various Chinese cities, collected and pressed specimens of a guelder-rose, which was to be named *Viburnum utile*, but he did not introduce the species to cultivation in Europe.

Collectors like Henry and Watters were amateurs, and they usually only had a single opportunity to visit a locality. Professional plant-hunters, who were employed to visit places in the flowering season and, most importantly, again when the plants bore ripe seeds, followed their trails. Thus, the person who gathered the seeds from many of Henry's discoveries as well as Watters's *Viburnum*, and who introduced these fine plants into our gardens, was Ernest Henry Wilson (1876–1930), a native of Gloucestershire – he soon acquired the nickname 'Chinese' Wilson. Wilson was first sent out to China in 1899 to undertake a secret mission, at Dr Henry's instigation: he was to gather the seeds of the 'wonderful' dove tree (*Davidia involucrata*, Pl. 82).

Lonicera tragophylla

The flowers of the golden honeysuckle are, unexpectedly, not scented: 'rather disgraceful for a Honeysuckle', commented Edward Augustus Bowles. This was one of several honeysuckle species discovered in the mountains of Hubei Province, China, by Dr Henry. It is a hardy climbing shrub but is not common in gardens.

Rubus lasiostylus

Ornamental raspberries with beautiful silver-grey canes are well worth growing in a winter garden. This hardy Chinese species is one of the small number of plants actually introduced into European gardens by Augustine Henry – seedlings raised at the Royal Botanic Gardens, Kew, first bloomed in 1894. For best effect, cut away the old stems in spring to encourage new growth.

Viburnum utile

This guelder-rose was named *utile* (useful) because its shoots were used in China to make stems for tobacco pipes. The species, which is a semi-evergreen, was first collected in 1880 near Yichang in Hubei province by Thomas Watters, a native of Newtownards, County Down. It was introduced to cultivation by Ernest Wilson in 1900.

NATIVES OF THE
NEW WORLD

Plants from temperate parts of North America have been cultivated in Irish gardens for three centuries at least, and species from South America have probably been grown for as long. The most familiar South American plant is undoubtedly the potato, although when it was first cultivated in Ireland is unknown. The story that the 'pratie' was introduced to Ireland by Sir Walter Raleigh is an unsubstantiated myth.

Ornamental plants from temperate South America which are grown in Irish gardens include the lovely relative of the mallow, *Abutilon vitifolium*. The history of its introduction is not recorded in detail, but it is believed to have flowered for the first time outside its native land in a Drumcondra garden.

A lot more is known about such plants as the pampas grass, which originally was named *Moorea* after David Moore (p. 213), because it was first raised in the Glasnevin Botanic Gardens. The seeds had been sent by John Tweedie (1775–1862), a Scottish plantsman, who was to supply the Botanic Gardens with hundreds of packets of seeds, as well as bulbs, orchids and cacti from Argentina, Brazil and Uruguay, between 1836 and 1857. Tweedie's name was given to the handsome turquoise-blossomed *Tweedia coerulea* 'in compliment to an intelligent and indefatigable collector'.

Over the centuries, numerous men and women with Irish connections who settled in the Americas contributed to knowledge of the flora of the New World. One of the earliest was Arthur Dobbs (1689–1765), whose family home is at Carrickfergus, County Antrim. Dobbs became Governor of North Carolina, and he was the first European to report the existence of the tippitiwitchet, later to be called Venus's flytrap.

Abutilon vitifolium

The original introduction of this moderately hardy shrub, which blossomed in Dublin during 1840, had white flowers slightly tinged with pink; darker mauve flowers are more typical. Captain Edward Cottingham, of Drumcondra, County Dublin, had obtained seeds from Chile in 1836, and subsequently distributed seedlings widely.

Dionaea muscipula

Venus's flytrap is a carnivorous plant which grows wild only in the eastern United States. Its leaves snap shut, trapping whatever insect or bug has touched one of the highly sensitive trigger-hairs on the hinged leaf-blade.

In 1759, after a plant-hunting excursion, Arthur Dobbs wrote to his friend, the Quaker naturalist Peter Collinson (1694–1768), reporting 'a kind of catch fly sensitive' – a tippitiwitchet.

Tweedia coerulea

When this trailing perennial was first described, it was identified as a species of *Tweedia*, a genus named after John Tweedie who had emigrated to Argentina in 1825. He had sent its seeds to Glasnevin Botanic Gardens where a plant blossomed for the first time during July 1837. It is not reliably hardy, but should flourish in a frost-free conservatory.

EVERLASTING

NAMES

When it comes to naming a new plant, the botanists who have to coin the names by which these are to be known universally often decide to pay tribute to colleagues or friends, living or dead. Naming a new plant after a fellow botanist or gardener has been a tradition for hundreds of years. As long as future botanists continue to regard the named plant as distinct that name will survive – an immortal memorial. The individual commemorated may have had no physical connection whatsoever with the eponymous plant; he or she may never even have seen it bloom.

Littonia, *Mackaya* and *Romneya* were named after three men who undoubtedly knew each other, and they all had connections to the University of Dublin. Thomas Romney Robinson and Samuel Litton were undergraduates. James Townsend Mackay was the gardener who created the renowned Trinity College Botanic Garden at Ballsbridge; the university bestowed an honorary doctorate on him in 1850.

The Latin names of plants and animals are composed of two words. The first one is the name of the genus to which the organism belongs: it resembles our surnames, and indicates the relationships between the constituent species. The second word, like our Christian names, will be unique within the genus: there cannot be two different species of *Littonia* called *modesta* nor two distinct *Romneya* called *coulteri*.

Littonia and *Mackaya* are native to South Africa and were cultivated in Dublin's botanic gardens during the nineteenth century. Litton never saw *Littonia modesta* in bloom; he probably never even examined dried specimens. *Mackaya bella* was named using a dried, pressed specimen, and again the person after whom it was named never saw it in fresh flower. Dr Robinson could have seen *Romneya coulteri* in blossom because it is known to have flowered in the Glasnevin Botanic Gardens in the summer of 1877.

Littonia modesta

Dr Samuel Litton (1781–1847), Professor of Botany to the Royal Dublin Society, was 'a deeply learned and amiable man', but rather shy and modest. He is commemorated by this unusual, 'modest' climbing lily from southern Africa. Litton's climbing bell is not reliably hardy and has to be grown indoors.

Littonia is similar to the more familiar climbing lily called *Gloriosa*, and recent studies indicate that they are closely related. Botanists working on these plants have proposed that Litton's genus should be submerged in *Gloriosa*, so this elegant, modest climber has been renamed *Gloriosa modesta*.

Mackaya bella

In Ireland, *Mackaya bella* is best grown in a conservatory or unheated glasshouse. James Townsend Mackay (1775–1862), after whom this south African genus was named, is also commemorated in Mackay's heath, *Erica mackayana* (Pl. 27). *Mackaya* is a sprawling shrub related to *Acanthus*.

Romneya coulteri

Dr Thomas Coulter (1793–1843) of Dundalk studied at Trinity College, County Louth, Dublin, and then spent more than a decade in Mexico and California. He collected numerous plants, some of which, including the big-cone pine, *Pinus coulteri*, were named after him.

The matilija, also named after his friend the astronomer Dr Thomas Romney Robinson (1792–1882), makes a superb garden plant.

LADIES AS
COLLECTORS

Plant hunting is not the preserve of men, although in the past fewer women had the opportunity to indulge in this hobby overseas, and none of Irish origin that I am aware of were professional collectors. At home in Ireland, several women have been keen botanists and have made significant contributions to the cataloguing of the native flora.

Miss Evelyn Booth (1897–1988) was an attentive amateur naturalist, a keen gardener and an expert fisherman. She wrote *The Flora of County Carlow*. I knew her well and enjoyed visiting her at Lucy's Wood. She was a wonderful raconteur with a sparkling sense of humour! Evelyn chanced to find a splendid blue wood anemone, recognized its worth and transplanted it into her garden.

Among the fine plants introduced by Irish women, there are a small number which came into cultivation as a result of holidays taken abroad. Miss Frances ('Fanny') Geoghegan came home to Donabate with at least two plants, both rare and both found only in the Balearic Islands. *Helleborus lividus* had been introduced to British gardens before 1790 so was not quite new, but the second of her finds, *Paeonia cambessedesii*, was entirely new.

Charlotte Isabel Wheeler Cuffe (1867–1967) had many opportunities to botanize when she lived in Burma, not least because her husband was an engineer in charge of public works. He often went into remote areas and Charlotte sometimes accompanied him. Her most exciting and important collections were from Natmataung (Mount Victoria) in western Burma. On the summit Charlotte Cuffe collected – and painted – gentians, anemones and rhododendrons, including a remarkable white-flowered species, which grows only on pine trees: it was named *Rhododendron cuffeanum*.

Anemone nemorosa 'Lucy's Wood'

Blue-flowered wood anemones sometimes occur in the wild, although the vast majority have white blossoms. Lucy's Wood is a copse in County Carlow, near Bunclody, and was where Miss Evelyn Booth found this lovely plant – her home was also called Lucy's Wood and the anemone flourished in its garden.

95

Helleborus lividus

This lovely perennial is an endangered species, native only on Mallorca in the Balearic Islands. While cultivated in England during the late eighteenth century, Fanny Geoghegan brought the species to Ireland in 1896 and distributed seedlings. It needs sunshine, some protection from persistent frost, and freely draining soil.

Rhododendron burmanicum

This was one of the three species of *Rhododendron* that inhabit the summit zone of Natmataung in the Chin Hills, Burma. In May 1911 Charlotte Cuffe visited the mountain and discovered this shrub. The following year she returned and collected some seedlings, and sent these to Glasnevin Botanic Gardens, where they bloomed in 1914.

SOMETHING OLD, SOMETHING NEW

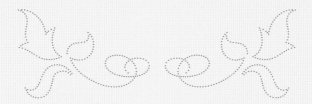

The earliest records of garden plants unique to Ireland, with their own distinctive names, date from the 1720s and 1730s. The first was a cider apple called 'Cackagee' (or 'Cockagee'), which had a greenish yellow skin and made good cider; the name appears to be an attempt to anglicize the unflattering but descriptive Irish phrase *cac a' ghéidh*, dung of goose. The following year five different potatoes were reported. A list headed 'An account of Auriculas ... Irish auriculas' that was compiled in 1736 at Kilruddery in County Wicklow contains names with distinctly Irish associations. Thus apples, potatoes and auriculas were most probably the first garden plants to be deliberately selected and named by Irish gardeners. The fact that a gardeners' society flourished briefly in Dublin during the 1740s, and awarded prizes for auriculas, is an interesting footnote, but whether 'Old Irish Blue' was around in the eighteenth century we cannot tell. It may not be so old, and it may not even be Irish. Wendy grew a large patch of it in her garden at Lusk, County Dublin, and it was an ideal subject for a watercolour.

We decided in the course of preparing the first set of paintings for *An Irish Florilegium* that we should include a new cultivar of Irish origin. While we could perhaps have chosen a daffodil or a rose, given that both daffodil and rose breeders were active in Ireland, an opportunity arose to include a new shrub which had connections back to extinct nurseries. *Potentilla* 'Sophie's Blush' was the plant. For the second volume we selected *Pelargonium* 'Koko' (Pl. 63) because it exemplified an entirely new way of creating garden plants, using a new technology.

New plants continue to be selected, propagated and named in Ireland, demonstrating that Irish gardeners remain appreciative of novelty even if some of these new cultivars are not to everyone's taste! Gardening is, after all, a very personal, opinionated hobby.

Primula × pubescens 'Old Irish Blue'

No one knows the origin of this auricula, although it is regarded as an antique garden variety of Irish origin. 'Old Irish Blue' is a tolerant, hardy perennial, and should be propagated regularly by division to maintain its vigour.

Potentilla 'Sophie's Blush'

Cultivars of shrubby cinquefoil can have flowers ranging from white (for example, 'Manchu') to cream and yellow, and even orange and red. 'Daydawn', introduced by the Slieve Donard Nursery in 1968, which has cream petals flushed pink, and 'Manchu' were probably the parents of 'Sophie's Blush', a chance seedling found in the garden at Baronscourt, County Tyrone.

Further Reading

K. Lamb and P. Bowe, *A History of Gardening in Ireland.* Dublin: National Botanic Gardens, Glasnevin, 1995

E. C. Nelson, *A Heritage of Beauty. The Garden Plants of Ireland: An illustrated encyclopaedia.* Dublin: Irish Garden Plant Society, 2001

E. C. Nelson, *Shamrock: Botany and history of an Irish myth.* Aberystwyth & Kilkenny: Boethius Press, 1991

E. C. Nelson and E. Deane, *'Glory of Donard': A history of the Slieve Donard Nursery, Newcastle, County Down, with a catalogue of cultivars.* Belfast: Northern Ireland Heritage Gardens Committee, 1993

E. C. Nelson and A. Grills, *Daisy Hill Nursery, Newry: A history of 'the most interesting nursery probably in the World'.* Belfast: Northern Ireland Heritage Gardens Committee, 1998

E. C. Nelson and E. M. McCracken, *The Brightest Jewel: A history of the National Botanic Gardens, Glasnevin, Dublin.* Kilkenny: Boethius Press, 1987

E. C. Nelson and B. Sayers, *Orchids of Glasnevin: An illustrated history of orchids in Ireland's National Botanic Gardens.* Dublin: Strawberry Tree, 2003

E. C. Nelson and W. F. Walsh, *The Burren: A companion to the wildflowers of an Irish limestone wilderness.* Dublin: Samton Ltd for The Conservancy of The Burren, 1997

E. C. Nelson and W. F. Walsh, *Trees of Ireland, Native and Naturalized.* Dublin: The Lilliput Press, 1993

E. C. Nelson and W. F. Walsh, *An Irish Flower Garden Replanted: The histories of some of our garden plants.* Castlebourke: Éamonn de Búrca for Edmund Burke Publisher, 1997

W. F. Walsh and E. C. Nelson, *A Prospect of Irish Flowers: Ten watercolour paintings.* Belfast: Blackstaff Press, 1990

W. F. Walsh, E. C. Nelson and N. Wilkinson, *A Lifetime of Painting: A memoir from notes made by Wendy Walsh and in conversation with Nick Wilkinson; [with] a suite of forty-four botanical plates with commentary by E. Charles Nelson.* Dublin: Strawberry Tree, 2007

Index